First World War
and Army of Occupation
War Diary
France, Belgium and Germany

50 DIVISION
Divisional Troops
A Squadron Yorkshire Hussars
4 April 1915 - 28 May 1916

WO95/2817/1

The Naval & Military Press Ltd
www.nmarchive.com
Published in association with The National Archives

Published by

The Naval & Military Press Ltd

Unit 10 Ridgewood Industrial Park,

Uckfield, East Sussex,

TN22 5QE England

Tel: +44 (0) 1825 749494

www.naval-military-press.com

www.nmarchive.com

This diary has been reprinted in facsimile from the original. Any imperfections are inevitably reproduced and the quality may fall short of modern type and cartographic standards.

© **Crown Copyright**
Images reproduced by permission of The National Archives, London, England, 2015.

Contents

Document type	Place/Title	Date From	Date To
Heading	WO95/2817-1		
Heading	50th Division 'A' Sqdn Yorkshire Hussars Apr 1915-May 1916.		
Heading	A Squadron Yorkshire Hussars (Divl Cavy: Instruction Divn) Vol I		
Miscellaneous	A.G. Base	07/05/1916	07/05/1916
War Diary		04/04/1915	29/04/1915
Heading	A Squad Yorkshire Hussars (50th Divl Coy) Vol II From 1st May To 22nd July 1915		
War Diary	Steenvoorde	01/05/1915	14/05/1915
War Diary	De Paul J	17/05/1915	25/05/1915
War Diary	Forge, 2 1/2mi Wsw Of Poperinghe	21/05/1915	21/05/1915
War Diary	Forge	22/05/1915	22/05/1915
War Diary	G H Q Trenches	23/05/1915	22/07/1915
War Diary	A. Squadron Yorkshire Hussars (50th Divl. Cav) Vol III From 1-31.8.15		
War Diary		01/08/1915	31/08/1915
Heading	50th Division A. Squadron Yorkshire Hussars (50th Divl. Cavalry) Vol IV Sept 15		
War Diary	St. Jans Cappel	01/09/1915	01/09/1915
Heading	50th Division A. Squadn Yorkshire Hussars Vol V Oct 15		
War Diary	St Jans Cappel	01/10/1915	29/10/1915
Heading	A Sqn Yorks Hus Nov. Vol VI		
War Diary		00/11/1915	00/11/1915
Heading	A Sq Yorkshire Hussars Dec Vol VII		
War Diary	Sheet 36a F11.a.4.3	01/12/1915	16/12/1915
War Diary	Sheet 27l.34.a.	17/12/1915	28/12/1915
War Diary	Wippenhoek Sh. 28. L 34 A 6.7.	01/02/1916	25/02/1916
War Diary	Wippenhoek	04/03/1916	31/03/1916
War Diary	Sheet 28.M.14 Central	01/04/1916	29/04/1916
War Diary	Godewearsvelde	04/05/1916	28/05/1916

3095/2817)

3095/2817)

50TH DIVISION

'A' SQDN YORKSHIRE HUSSARS

APR 1915 - MAY 1916.

TO 17 CORPS.

12/5/94

50
Northumbrian Division

"A" Squadron Yorkshire Hussars
(Div: Cavalry: Northumbrian Div.)
Vol I 4 — 29. 4. 15

A.G.
Base

Herewith War Diary for April, for
"A" Squadron - Yorkshire Hussars.
delay regretted.

7/5/16

G. R. Lane Fox
Major. Yorkshire Hussars

Yorkshire Hussars
"A" Squadron - with Machine Gun Section & Bodyguard.

Army Form C. 2118.

WAR DIARY
or
INTELLIGENCE SUMMARY
(Erase heading not required.)

Instructions regarding War Diaries and Intelligence Summaries are contained in F. S. Regs., Part II. and the Staff Manual respectively. Title pages will be prepared in manuscript.

Hour, Date, Place	Summary of Events and Information	Remarks and references to Appendices
1915 April. April 17 -	Orders received to proceed abroad as Divisional Cavalry to the Northumbrian Div. T.F. Leave Harlow - in two parties - arrive Southampton in afternoon - cross in S.S. African Prince & Trentfield to Havre	
18 8.30 am	Arrive Havre - draw equipment - stable horse for night. Whole squadron now together, with Gun section & Bodyguard -	
19 2.30 am	March to Gare des Marchandises Point 1 - entrain -	
20 5.0 am	arrive Hazebrouck - detrain - march to STEENVOORDE - billeted at GOEIEWILUCK Farm.	
22	Division ordered to move to Poperinghe - Squadron to start at 4 - orders cancelled	
23 -	Orders to stand by. Ready to start.	
25	One troop at a time detailed for road control during movement of troops in neighbourhood of STEENVOORDE.	
29	Lent 160 Heavy Draught Horses from GODEWAERSVELDE to Canadian Division on POPERINGHE - ELVERDINGHE road -	

1247 W 3290 200,000 (E) 8/14 J.B.C. & A. Form/C. 2118/11.

D/6410

50th Division

"A" Squad Yorkshire Hussars (50th Divl Cavy)

Vol II

From 1st May to 22nd July 1915

Army Form C. 2118.

WAR DIARY
or
INTELLIGENCE SUMMARY
(Erase heading not required.)

Yorkshire Hussars
"A" Sqdn. with R.J. Holm + Headquarters

Hour, Date, Place	Summary of Events and Information	Remarks and references to Appendices
1915. May 1. STEENVOORDE.	Take 100 men to GODEWAERSVELDE to meet Canadians. Take 290 dismounts to H.Quarters N.J VLAMERTINGHE — Northumbrian Div. at STEENVOORDE.	
3 "	One foot patrol Harmounts from ARNEKE & H.Qr. detailed for Road control — Archies & troops to BOPERINGHE 6:25ᵗʰ Div: from GODEWAERSVELDE.	
5. "	Take 127 men — army 266 dismounts to BOPERINGHE.	
7. "	Take 80 men long 97 horses from HAZEBROUCK & H.Qr. Northumbrian Div: at STEENVOORDE.	
10. "	Ordered to stand by ready to move at 2 hrs notice.	
11. "	Road patrols VLAMERTINGHE — POPERINGHE road — rest of Squadron later. Northumbrian Div: HQrs moved to POPERINGHE.	
12. "	Rain in front of Ypres.	
14. "	Orders received to search Headquarters & R.J. Holm from Squadron + send them back to BASE — also this flies them to POPERINGHE and rest needs dismounts at ARNEKE.	
17. DE PANNE.	Squadron moves from billets at DE PANNE — now BERINGHE. Leaving Headquarters + R.J. rotor — We are placed under 3rd Cavalry Div: as body Cavalry Corps Reserve.	
19. "	Squad Told off for daily Patrol duty of POPERINGHE — VLAMERTINGHE road 16 men. Told off 2nd Cavalry Div: from 3rd: ditto. Ordered to ready move at 1½ hrs notice	
21. "	Sq. Transferred to Bays — (g.O.C. Cavalry Corps.) — to proceed at once to night + assist Gen. Bays — (g.O.C. Cavalry Corps.) — to proceed at once to YPRES trenches — occupy + repair for defence section of G.H.Q. line J. G. MENIN road — Road patrols duty taken from us. Route J. G. MENIN road — YPRES — trenches under L¹ DORINGTON. Squad mounted to YPRES — there occupy trench under cover of darkness.	
22 "	L¹ 68 men + 5 officers drawn. YPRES occupy trench and cover J darkness. Waited day with Northumbrian Div. ⁴/ Gd Div. ⁴/ Strengthening + retaining trenches. Fought from 3 a.m. till evening. 2 wounded (⁴/ Fletcher + Shoe C)	
23. "	Trenches subjected heavy shelling, difficult sit: our army in bad ⁴/ plight — (⁴/ Day lost)	
24 "	To VLAMERTINGHE — return some men dalley — two men killed (Col⁴/ Lamb, R¹ Homes Ireland (⁴/ Jefferyfield, R¹ Reim grooms)	
25. "	Heavy german attack.	O.R. wounded. (⁴/ field Major Cooper line Pte/wounded and 1 officer & R.H.A. being helped to move — before shell fire — with)

WAR DIARY or INTELLIGENCE SUMMARY

Army Form C. 2118.

Hour, Date, Place	Summary of Events and Information	Remarks and references to Appendices
1915		
FORGE, 2½ mi WSW of POPERINGHE. May 21.	Major Lawe-Fox sent for by General Byng (Cdg 2nd Cav. Corps) & receives orders to take Squadron up to reserve line of trenches 1¼ mi. E of YPRES (on YPRES–MENIN road) the following evening.	
FORGE May 22.	The Squadron (Maj. Lawe Fox, Capt Deakin, Lt Walker, 2Lts Haslam, Darrington, Turnbull, & 94 NCOs & men) march out of Camp 8·30 pm going via POPERINGHE – VLAMERTINGHE to X rds 1 mi W of YPRES where the Squadron is dismounted & the led horses sent back under 2Lt Darrington. The rest of the Squadron walk through YPRES on to the YPRES – MENIN road and arrive at the GHQ trenches at 2 am without incident.	The Squadron during the *précéding* (May 22-25) were attached to the 2nd Cav Brigade, 2nd Cav. Division.
GHQ Trenches May 23.	Squadron employed all day digging & improving trenches, badly made by French troops.	
GHQ Trenches May 24.	Squadron is turned out of trenches at 2 am by XIXth Hussars – who have been ordered unexpectedly up in reserve – & is allotted another section of GHQ trenches further S & is attached to 2nd Cav. Bde under Brigadier General Greenley. At 3 am German attack begins – the firing line being badly gassed & a certain amt of gas coming over GHQ trenches & respirators being put on for a short time – & the Squadron is under heavy shell fire from 3 am to midnight – casualties 2 men killed, 1 wounded.	
GHQ Trenches May 25.	At 7·30 am Squadron receives orders to leave trenches & return to Camp. 1st Troop (Lt R. Walker) receives orders to leave trenches at 9 am & to take back Squadron waterkart left at railway level crossing & X rds on MENIN–YPRES road. Major Lawe-Fox is in front of Troop to shew position of waterkart. The Troop immediately on arriving	

WAR DIARY
or
INTELLIGENCE SUMMARY

(Erase heading not required.)

Army Form C. 2118.

Hour, Date, Place	Summary of Events and Information	Remarks and references to Appendices
May 25 (cont'd).	at x176 on MENIN-YPRES road comes under heavy shell fire and loses 3 men killed & 3 wounded. Major Lawe-Fox is slightly wounded in shoulder. I evacuated home. The rest of the Squadron under Capt Deakin retires [illegible] under heavy shell fire — without losing any casualties — by route S. of YPRES — rallying at Asylum on YPRES — VLAMERTINGHE road. Lt Douglas is ordered to bring horses to VLAMERTINGHE & the Squadron arrives back in camp at FORGE at 7 p.m.	
May 30.	Squadron transferred & attached to 3rd Cavalry Division (V.th Corps)	

Army Form C. 2118.

'A' Sqn Yorks Hussars

WAR DIARY
or
INTELLIGENCE SUMMARY
(Erase heading not required.)

Instructions regarding War Diaries and Intelligence
Summaries are contained in F. S. Regs., Part II.
and the Staff Manual respectively. Title pages
will be prepared in manuscript.

Hour, Date, Place	Summary of Events and Information	Remarks and references to Appendices
June 3.	(Amiens) 1 Corporal & 8 men ordered to report to APM II Corps for permanent police duty.	These men are sent to the ½ Squadron on June 21 & ½ Squadron detail men to replace them.
June 4.	2Lt Donington brings 50 horses from CAESTRE with orders to keep them in our lines until further instructions.	
June 6.	50 remounts distributed to various units.	
June 7.	1 Cpl. 8–9 men ordered to report to APM 50th Div. for permanent police duty.	
June 8.	Squadron moves to new billet at G.33.6.5–8 (near RENINGHELST,	
June 9.	50 remounts met at CAESTRE & brought back to our lines.	
June 9–10.	Capt Deakin receives orders to do reconnaissance work & check all roads & tracks leading up to 50th Div trenches. Capt Deakin, Lt Walker, Harbour, Douglas, Turnbull with 1 section/troop complete the above orders	
June 11.	2Lt Turnbull leaves Squadron to join RE.	
June 12.	Squadron orders to send 50 men as digging party & bury cattle near H.18 d.10.5 sheet 28.	
June 13.	Same duty as June 12.	
June 14.	Squadron marches to POPERINGHE & bathes.	
June 15.	Ordered same duty as on June 12 – 13.	
June 16.	Squadron moves into new billet at G.32.a.c sheet 28.	
June 18.		
June 19.	One division (50th) receive orders to hand over their area to the 46th (N. Midlands) Division & to move into area occupied by N. M. Division. Arrangements made for 'A' Squadron 1/1 to exchange billets with 1/5 Squadron 1/1.	
June 22.	The Squadron move into 1/5 Sqdn billet arriving 7 pm. 'B' Sqdn march out at midnight. Officers of two Squadrons mess together. (SEMETER, GOETHALS, JEONIE HÉMAR) The Sqdn is allotted 3 farms	This exchange of areas puts 50th Division under command of 2nd Army Corps (Ferguson).

Army Form C. 2118.

WAR DIARY
or
INTELLIGENCE SUMMARY
(Erase heading not required.)

1915

Hour, Date, Place	Summary of Events and Information	Remarks and references to Appendices
July 1.		
July 2 – 7	Capt Deakin sent for by Major General, Earl of Cavan, Cdg 50th Division.	
	Orders received to send digging parties of 28 men to dig at GHQ line of trenches (at N27C 8-3 sheet 28) to work from 9 am to 1½ pm.	
(July 6)	G.O.C. sends message complimenting 'A' Squadron on the work done	
July 8-9	Orders received to dig trenches to bury wires 400 x E of WULVERGHEN. Rendezvous at BUS FARM (on LINDENHOEK – NEUVE EGLISE road) at 6 am. Draw tools at SOUVENIR FARM. – WULVERGHEN village in ruins & is shelled during the morning. Horses left at N32C2-5 sheet 28.	
July 10.	Dig trenches to bury wires at N34 b9 sheet2 & near POND FARM. Party (under Lts Walker & Haslam) fired on by machine gun – no casualties.	
July 13.	39 HD remounts brought from remount depot in CAESTRE – LE BRIAND road by Lts Haslam & Doringtin and delivered to remount units. Party nearly caught by a shell on DRANOUTRE – NEUVE EGLISE road.	
July 14.	Digging party (under Lts Walker & Doringtin) dig trenches to bury wires on E side of KEMMEL hill. (N26 b5-55 sheet 28)	
July 16.	50 remounts met at BAILLEUL station. Remounts distributed to various units.	
July 17.		
July 19.	1 officer (Major) & 7 men sent to APM. 50th Division at Armentières.	July 18-20. Division (50th) moves into new area, near Armentières
July 21.	Squadron moves into new divisional area. Billeted at Pont de Nieppe. No accommodation for men, who bivouac outside. Officers at Brewery.	
July 22.	Major Lumsden & 2Lt Howard arrive from England	

121/6598

50th Division

A. Squadron Yorkshire Hussars
(50th Div. Cav)

Vol III

from 1 - 31. 8. 15

Third

Army Form C. 2118.

"A" Squadron
Yorkshire Hussars
Divisional Mounted Troops of 50th Division

WAR DIARY
or
INTELLIGENCE SUMMARY

(Erase heading not required.)

Instructions regarding War Diaries and Intelligence Summaries are contained in F. S. Regs., Part II. and the Staff Manual respectively. Title pages will be prepared in manuscript.

Hour, Date, Place	Summary of Events and Information	Remarks and references to Appendices
August		
1	Billeted in PONT DE NIEPPE. additional 29 men acting as mounted Police for the Division in ARMENTIÈRES. besides 8 orderlies detailed to Brigades. Also 20 casualties, unmounted sick, etc. Shortage of strength. In reduced available for duty to such small numbers that Squadron is very unhelpful tool. Nothing beyond during the month is consequence - received at PONT DE NIEPPE receiving num. horses, mainly in riding school.	
26	till - moved billet to ½ mile S. of S. JANS CAPPEL. on road from there to BAILLEUL - Same billet that we had before on July 21.	
31.	nothing further to record.	

G. Palmer Jim
Major.

50th Division

6971/12

"A" Squadron Yorkshire Hussars
(50th Div: Cavalry)

Vol IV

Sept. 15

WAR DIARY
INTELLIGENCE SUMMARY
(Erase heading not required.)

Army Form C. 2118.

Hour, Date, Place	Summary of Events and Information	Remarks and references to Appendices
ST. JANS CAPPEL September 1.	Yorkshire Hussars "A" Squadron (Divisional Cavalry) 50th Divn. B.E.F.	
24.	Started building stabling & mens quarters for men & horses at billet.	
	moved to PONT DE NIEPPE in view of possible advance of Divn.	
	nothing further occurred.	
	G.R. dene Fox Major	

121/7429

50th Division

A. Genl's Lotkshire Hussars
Vol V
Oct 15

Army Form C. 2118.

WAR DIARY
or
INTELLIGENCE SUMMARY
(Erase heading not required.)

Yorkshire Hussars - Birthcavalry of 50th Div.
"A" Squadron.

Hour, Date, Place	Summary of Events and Information	Remarks and references to Appendices
ST JANS CAPPEL October 1.	Division in trenches. Squadron billeting sheds – tin huts & training in reconnaissance – reporting – patrolling &c. Forty two men detailed as extra M.M.P. 50th Division in ARMENTIERES – have not enough to do anything.	
" 20.	Draft of 23 recruits arrived from the 2/1st Regt in England	
24	Moved to new billets. S.Eg MERRIS.	

G Palmer for
Major, Yorkshire Hussars

Army Form C. 2118.

WAR DIARY
or
INTELLIGENCE SUMMARY

Yorkshire Hussars "A" Squadron
Div. Cav. to 50th Division

(Erase heading not required.)

Hour, Date, Place	Summary of Events and Information	Remarks and references to Appendices
November 1915	Nothing to report. Division resting — Training when weather permitted.	

G. R. Lane Fox
Major

"A" fl.
Jonkereinz svarano

Dag/vad. VII

12/7954

50 K/h

WAR DIARY or INTELLIGENCE SUMMARY

(Erase heading not required.)

Army Form C. 2118

"A" Squadron
Yorkshire Hussars.
Div. Cavalry. 50th Division. B.E.F.

Place	Date 1915	Hour	Summary of Events and Information	Remarks and references to Appendices
Sheet 36a F.11.a.43	Dec 1		50th Division resting in MERRIS area –	
	15		50 Divn. before move in to new area – relieving 6th Divn. in DICKEBUSCH sector –	
	16		Squadron moves billet to Sheet 27 - L.34.a.	
Sheet 27 L.34.a.	17		8 men & N.C.O. detailed as H.Q. P. & R. Corps – 12 N.C.O's men detailed to patrol Belgian frontier –	
	19		Ordered to stand to ready to form on Gas attack & bombardment – which has not pressed	
	21		4 mounted Orderlies & 4 dismounted detailed daily for use at Div.H.Q. 6 A.M.P. detailed under A.P.M. 50 Div.	
	22		Ordered to thoroughly reconnoitre new area – their guides did not any staywright out	
	28		Ordered make a census of supplies of Hay – Straw & vegetables in STEENVOORDE – CASSEL – OUDEZEELE – WINNEZEELE area –	

G.R. Lane Fox
Major Yorkshire Hussars

Army Form C. 2118

WAR DIARY
or
INTELLIGENCE SUMMARY
(Erase heading not required.)

"A" Squadron
Yorkshire Hussars
Div. Cav. 50th Division
1916

Place	Date	Hour	Summary of Events and Information	Remarks and references to Appendices
WIPPENHOEK Feb 1 SH.28. L.34.a.6.7.			Three men detailed to act as observers for 50th Div in front line trenches. Given detail as R.A.P. & A.P.M. Clerks.	
		10	" " " " 50th Div.	
		5	" " " mounted orderlies to 50th Div. 3 Daily	
		4	" " " dismounted orderlies " " 3 Daily	
		12	" " " Frontier patrols.	
			Squadron being trained in bombing & in detonating & handling of the bombs.	
	25		Eight men attached to "L" Brigade H.Q. to be trained as Snipers and then over in rear area of trenches of 50th Div.	

J.R. ???
Major, Yorkshire Hussars

Army Form C. 2118

WAR DIARY
or
INTELLIGENCE SUMMARY
(Erase heading not required.)

1916

"A" Squadron
Yorkshire Hussars
Div. Cav. 50th Div.

Place	Date	Hour	Summary of Events and Information	Remarks and references to Appendices
WIPPENHOEK	March 4		Eight men detailed as guides to trenches return to Squadron	
	18		Captain Deakin left the Squadron to take on the command of the 4th Yorks. Regt.	
	24		6 men under N.C.O. detailed as Observers for 2nd Canadian Div. Area - which the 50th Div. are taking over.	
	31		Have Squadron Trenches in the 2nd Canadian Div. Area at WESTOUTRE - Sheet 28. M.14 Central	

G.R. Lane Fox
Major, Yorkshire Hussars

Army Form C. 2118

WAR DIARY
or
INTELLIGENCE SUMMARY
(Erase heading not required.)

1916

"A" Squadron
Yorkshire Hussars. Div. Cav. 5th & 6th Div.

Place	Date	Hour	Summary of Events and Information	Remarks and references to Appendices
Sheet 28. M.14 Central	April 1st		13 men employed daily patrolling Belgian frontier. Squadron Observers carrying out the Divisional observation with Cyclists. All train movement observation from KEMMEL Hill being done by Observers & French Cavalry detached Scouts after party of 2nd line Scouts.	
	27		Squadron moved to fresh billets near GODEWAERSVELDE — the Division having come out of Observers still down also French Cavalry — relieve to Squadron. Instructions notifying all observed vehicles.	
	29		Start some Squadron training. Leaving for the firing line for remainder of the Squadron together.	

G. Roane for
Major.

WAR DIARY
or
INTELLIGENCE SUMMARY
(Erase heading not required.)

Army Form C. 2118

"A" Squadron.
Yorkshire Hussars.
Div. Cav. to 47, 50 & Division.

Places	Date	Hour	Summary of Events and Information	Remarks and references to Appendices
GODENERSVELDE	1916 May 4		Warned to leave 50th Division shortly – Squadron to join "B" Sqdn. Yorks Hussars Divisional Cavalry 1st joined up with the two squadrons of Yorkshire Hussars as a Regiment of Corps Cavalry attached to XVII Corps 3rd Army	Vol 15
	9	6 a.m.	Move from billets – March 25 miles South to BURBURE. Billets tres inpt.	
	10	8 a.m.	March from BURBURE via ST. POL – and reach GOUY EN TERNOIS – where the other two squadrons have already arrived – Yorkshire Hussars a Regiment once more – under command of Major FLEY – until further appointment made.	
	11		Training under Captain LOCKETT 17th Lancers.	
	13		Field Day – Yorkshire Hussars attacking line held by cyclists	
	14		Training in cavalry work continues.	
	27		Regiment informed that Major PEPYS Lt. Col. 13th Hussars has been appointed to command	
	28		Lt. R.B. Laike gazetted Captain – & Lt. Knighton Lieut –	

E. Adams for
Major.

www.ingramcontent.com/pod-product-compliance
Lightning Source LLC
Chambersburg PA
CBHW081505160426

43193CB00014B/2596